THE HATCH ACT

A Civil Libertarian Defense

John R. Bolton

American Enterprise Institute for Public Policy Research
Washington, D. C.

John R. Bolton is engaged in the private practice of law in Washington, D. C.

ISBN 0-8447-3202-8

Domestic Affairs Study 43, January 1976

Library of Congress Catalog Card No. 76-494

Printed in the United States of America

CONTENTS

THE HATCH ACT

Introduction

The Hatch Act was originally passed in 1939.[1] It has been the subject of three major challenges before the Supreme Court [2] and almost continuous congressional debate since its enactment.[3] Now the Congress is considering legislation that would effectively eliminate almost all restrictions on the participation of federal employees in partisan political activity.[4]

The heart of the act is section 9(a),[5] which prohibits employees of executive agencies from using their "official authority or influence"

---

[1] The provisions of the Hatch Act, 53 Stat. 1147, now codified at 5 U.S.C., sections 7321-27, originally applied only to federal employees. In 1940, coverage of the act was extended to certain state and local officials as well, 54 Stat. 767, 5 U.S.C., sections 1501-08. Here only the restraints on federal employees will be considered, although much of what is said would clearly apply to governmental employees below the federal level.

[2] United Public Workers v. Mitchell, 330 U.S. 75 (1947); Oklahoma v. Civil Service Comm'n, 330 U.S. 127 (1947); Civil Service Comm'n v. Letter Carriers, 413 U.S. 548 (1972); Broadrick v. Oklahoma, 413 U.S. 601 (1973), a companion case to *Letter Carriers*, upheld against constitutional challenge a provision of the state of Oklahoma's "little Hatch Act."

[3] The most recent revision, part of the Federal Election Campaign Act Amendments of 1974, 88 Stat. 1263, 2 U.S.C., sections 431 *et seq.*, eliminated certain federally imposed restrictions applicable to state and local employees.

[4] H.R. 8617, 94th Congress, 1st session (1975), passed the House of Representatives by a vote of 288 to 119, *Congressional Record*, vol. 121 (daily ed., October 21, 1975), p. H 10162. Although public attention is once again focused on the legislative branch, considerable attention is paid herein to Supreme Court opinions, not alone for constitutional theory, but because in those opinions the arguments in the Hatch Act debate have been the most persuasive, the most sophisticated, and the least partisan.

[5] 5 U.S.C., section 7324(a).

1

to interfere with or affect the results of an election, or from taking "an active part in political management or in political campaigns." Federal employees are also barred from coercing the political action of others.[6] Government employees are permitted to express their opinions on political subjects and candidates, and they may engage in nonpartisan political activity.[7]

Much of the congressional debate over the Hatch Act since it was first proposed has been substantially motivated by overtly political considerations. Obscured by the often shrill partisanship of the legislative debate, however, are important issues of democratic theory and individual civil liberties. The central question today, as in 1939, is whether justifiable reasons exist for treating federal employees differently from other citizens with regard to freedom to engage in political activity. The answer to that question has important implications not only for the government workers affected, but for the public at large as well.

Several arguments have been advanced in defense of the Hatch Act, and those employed the most often have usually been the least satisfactory. Intellectually, the act's opponents have dominated the continuing debate, and yet the statute's central provisions have remained largely unaffected. Essentially four arguments have been advanced in defense of the act, arguments which are often overlapping, indistinct, and confused.

The desire to eliminate corruption—which at its core has meant the desire to prevent the explicit exchange of government favors in return for something of value—has often been stressed by the act's proponents. They have also emphasized that the efficiency and professionalism of the civil service require that it be divorced from partisan politics. While both of these contentions involve valid public concerns, neither justifies broad prohibitions against the political activities of Americans—activities that are fundamental to our constitutional system.

The fact is that a strong civil libertarian defense of the Hatch Act can and should be made. Although its opponents argue that the act restricts the political freedom of federal employees, they fail to recognize the important First Amendment values supporting restraints on the partisan activities of such employees. Government workers have a right to be free from political coercion—particularly from any systematic solicitation by either their superiors or their co-workers. Since the power to coerce derives in substantial amount from power

---

[6] Ibid., section 7322.
[7] Ibid., sections 7324(b), 7326.

2

vested in the government, the Hatch Act is, in effect, a case of the government restraining itself. Non-governmental employees have similar First Amendment rights—the right not to have their freedom to engage in political activity "chilled" by political activists who also administer government programs and regulatory or law-enforcement agencies. As Professor Meiklejohn asserted, "The First Amendment does not protect a 'freedom to speak.' It protects the freedom of those activities of thought and communication by which we 'govern.' It is concerned, not with a private right, but with a public power, a governmental responsibility."[8] The most acute government responsibility is that government not allow itself to be used to skew the political process. The political debate can never be "uninhibited, robust, and wide-open"[9] if government employees can coerce their colleagues or intimidate the general public. When viewed as an inhibitor imposed on the government itself, the Hatch Act is as justifiable as other restrictions—judicially or legislatively created—that prevent the government from regulating the "free market" of ideas.

1. The Prevention of Corruption

Beyond question, the major stated reason for passage of the Hatch Act was to prevent corruption of the type reportedly widespread during the 1938 election campaigns,[10] and revealed by Senate investigations chaired by Senator Morris Sheppard (Democrat, Texas).[11] Although supporters of the proposal by Senator Carl Hatch (Democrat, N. Mex.) often indiscriminately joined corruption and coercion together,[12] this section deals only with corruption in the sense of bribery, graft, and personal profiteering. Coercion of public employees, discussed below (Section 3), is viewed most accurately as penalizing or threatening to penalize employees who refuse to engage in political activity, without regard to whether the coercer is enriched by his actions. Thus, requiring "kickbacks" in exchange for jobs is

8 Alexander Meiklejohn, "The First Amendment as an Absolute," *Supreme Court Review, 1961*, pp. 245, 255.

9 New York Times v. Sullivan, 376 U.S. 254 (1964).

10 Paul P. Van Riper, *History of the United States Civil Service* (1958), p. 340.

11 See, for example, *Report of the Special Committee to Investigate Senatorial Campaign Expenditures and Use of Governmental Funds in 1938*, 76th Congress, 1st session (1939) Part I, p. 11 (hereinafter, *Report of the Special Committee*).

12 See, for example, remarks of Representative Hamilton Fish (Republican, New York), *Congressional Record*, vol. 84 (July 20, 1939), p. 9601, and Representative U. S. Guyer (Republican, Ohio), ibid., p. 9600.

accurately classified as corruption, while requiring attendance at political rallies is more properly viewed as coercion.

A contemporary observer, examining the special committee's over four hundred page report, would not likely find the kind of massive and pervasive corruption one might have expected. Indeed, were it not for the congressional pyrotechnics, one might well wonder why any close attention to corruption was warranted at all. The Supreme Court, however, has made it plain that congressional judgments about the effect of corruption on federal employees will not be re-examined as part of the process of judicial review:

> When actions of civil servants in the judgment of Congress menace the integrity and the competency of the [public] service, legislation to forestall such danger and adequate to maintain its usefulness is required. The Hatch Act is the answer of Congress to this need. We cannot say . . . that these restrictions are unconstitutional.[13]

In *Civil Service Commission* v. *Letter Carriers*, the Court reaffirmed this view by noting with approval congressional fears of corrupt political machines emanating from the government's bureaucracy, and candidly stating: "Perhaps Congress at some time will come to a different view of the realities of political life and Government service; but that is its current view of the matter, and we are not now in any position to dispute it."[14]

The Supreme Court's attitude on this subject leaves much to be desired—there are numerous areas of activity in which pervasive regulation could be justified once the specter of corruption has been invoked. Undoubtedly, the Supreme Court's view was much affected by statements such as those of Representative Robert Ramspeck (Democrat, Georgia) during the 1939 debate: ". . . I believe that the thing that is going to destroy this Nation, if it is destroyed, is political corruption, based upon traffic in jobs and in contracts, by political parties and factions in power."[15] Any court in a democratic society is understandably reluctant to second-guess such statements made by "experts" in the political process. Nonetheless, it is precisely because legislators have such an enormous stake in their own re-elections and those of their like-minded colleagues that remarks such as those of Representative Ramspeck ought not be accepted at face value when a statute undergoes judicial scrutiny. If such acceptance were to be-

---

[13] United Public Workers v. Mitchell, 330 U.S. 75, 103 (1947).

[14] 413 U.S. 548, 565 (1973).

[15] *Congressional Record*, vol. 84 (July 20, 1939), p. 9616.

come commonplace where First Amendment freedoms are affected, those freedoms would be in serious jeopardy.

Barring any sudden reversal by a majority of the Court, congressional decisions about eliminating corruption will be accepted. It is, therefore, particularly important for the legislators to appreciate the values at stake when the prevention of official corruption is advanced as a rationale for limiting the participation in politics of several million federal employees.

The plain truth is that there is insufficient evidence of corruption or the possibility of corruption to justify the significant interference with freedom of political activity the Hatch Act embodies. Neither in the 1939 and 1940 debates nor in the recent House debate on H.R. 8617 did Hatch Act proponents present a convincing case that corruption was endemic in the federal bureaucracy.[16] Reasonable people can, of course, disagree on what level of corruption necessitates what magnitude of legislative response. Even if the level of corruption were or were likely to become significantly higher than proponents of the Hatch Act contend—indeed even if it were as high as the 1939 supporters of Senator Hatch's bill believed—it would still not provide a justifiable basis for the Hatch Act's restrictions on political activity and association. As Mr. Justice Black warned in his *Mitchell* dissent:

> It is argued that it is in the interest of clean politics to suppress political activities of federal and state employees. It would hardly seem to be imperative to muzzle millions of citizens because some of them, if left their constitutional freedoms, might corrupt the political process. All political corruption is not traceable to state and federal employees. Therefore, it is possible that other groups may later be compelled to sacrifice their right to participate in political activities for the protection of the purity of the Government of which they are a part.[17]

If corruption is a serious problem and not a code word for other concerns, then it is to corruption that Congress should address itself. It should determine precisely what forms of improper activity are occurring, define with care the conduct it wishes to proscribe, and

---

[16] See generally *Report of the Special Committee*, and *Hearings before the Subcommittee on Employee Political Rights and Intergovernmental Programs of the House Committee on Post Office and Civil Service on H.R. 3000*, 94th Congress, 1st session (1975), Parts I and II (hereinafter, *Hearings on H.R. 3000*). (H.R. 3000 was a predecessor to H.R. 8617 which eventually passed the House of Representatives.)

[17] 330 U.S. 75, 112-13 (Black, J., dissenting).

ensure to the best of its ability through adequate funding and staffing that the agency charged with enforcing the anti-corruption laws does in fact enforce them. All other forms of activity—and particularly forms of activity replete with First Amendment implications—should remain permissible. Even if defining "corruption" seems extremely difficult, it is by no means an intractable problem. There is no convincing reason why the intellectual rigor required for an exact definition should be forsaken for the easy alternative of a broad-brush prohibition.[18]

When political activity is circumscribed, it should be only after failure of other means that intrude less drastically on freedoms of speech and association. This is not only a wise constitutional doctrine, but prudent advice for Congress as well. Even as here, where the Supreme Court has recently sustained a statute's constitutionality, if Congress can achieve its goals by narrower means, it by all means should do so. If corruption alone were the target of the Hatch Act, that goal could not justify prohibitions as broad as those in the statute.

2. Maintaining "Efficiency" and "Professionalism"

The notion of "efficiency" has been given considerable prominence in the Hatch Act debates. The term is not intended to be coextensive with the prevention of employee coercion or the impartial and unbiased administration of the laws.[19] Instead, it encompasses two separate concerns: first, that the productivity and achievements of the civil service will be diminished or impaired if employees are

---

[18] Although it is not within the scope of this study to provide the proper statutory definition of corrupt activities, there are clearly certain activities that fall within any minimally effective prohibition. Where, for example, there is an explicit quid pro quo arrangement—a promise or delivery of private benefit in exchange for governmental action—Congress clearly can intervene. See United States v. Brewster, 408 U.S. 501 (1972). Beyond such core infractions, however, the legislature must proceed with considerable care. The prudent course would perhaps entail, in the first instance, an *under*inclusive list of proscribed activities, to which additions could be made as new evidence of improper conduct arose. Concededly, some costs would be incurred in terms of corrupt practices that would escape proscription, but the benefits in terms of enhanced civil liberties that would accrue more than justify such a procedure. Perhaps the most troublesome aspect of this recommendation is that it requires a Congress sufficiently aware of its responsibilities to eschew the "easy" road of generalized prohibitions and to maintain its span of attention on the problem for more than one legislative session.

[19] These issues will be discussed in the two subsequent sections. To the extent that "inefficiency" entails employee coercion or a chilling effect on those affected by governmental agencies, of course, different questions arise. The present section examines "inefficiency" as an alleged vice in itself.

permitted to engage in political activity; and second, that whether or not there is any impact on the bureaucracy's work, it is simply improper (almost as a matter of professional "ethics") for federal employees to engage in partisan political activities.[20]

The Supreme Court stated unequivocally in *Mitchell* that the Hatch Act's "interference with free expression is seen in better proportion as compared with the requirements of orderly management of administrative personnel." The Court noted with considerable approval ". . . the growth of the principle of required political neutrality for classified public servants as a sound element for efficiency," and concluded that if Congress and the President (those "responsible for an efficient public service") judged that "efficiency may be best obtained by prohibiting active participation by classified employees in politics as party officers or workers, we see no constitutional objection." [21]

In *Letter Carriers*, the Court quoted in support of its decision a passage from *Pickering* v. *Board of Education:* [22]

> The problem in any case is to arrive at a balance between the interests of the [employee], as a citizen, in commenting upon matters of public concern and the interest of the [government], as an employer, in promoting the efficiency of the public services it performs through its employees.[23]

During the present debate over possible evisceration of the Hatch Act, one witness argued that the matter, at

> its most fundamental level . . . addresses itself to the extraordinarily delicate balance between individual political

---

[20] Dr. Clyde J. Wingfield (president of the Bernard M. Baruch College of the City University of New York) stated that "[f]or the Public Service to conduct itself in the highest professional manner, it remains . . . desirable that it be protected from the encroachments of partisan politics. . . ." *Congressional Record*, vol. 121 (daily ed., November 17, 1975), p. S 20210. This position essentially involves a desire to avoid the return of a "spoils system" rather than a "merit system" within the civil service. The anti-spoils system arguments are appropriately considered in this section rather than in the preceding section on corruption because changes in administrations could involve massive non-corrupt changes in the bureaucracy based solely on the concept that the new "ins" have a mandate from the electorate to remove the old "ins" from control of the levers of executive power. Such was certainly Andrew Jackson's original intention. So too was the so-called "Malek Plan," developed by a high official in the Nixon administration to bring the civil service—presumed by many in the Nixon White House to be antagonistic to the President's program—"under control." See, for example, Testimony of Dr. Nathan T. Wolkomir in *Hearings on H.R. 3000*, p. 142.

[21] 330 U.S. 75, 94, 97, 99.

[22] 391 U.S. 563, 568 (1968).

[23] 413 U.S. 548, 564 (bracketed material in the original).

[freedom] on the one hand, and those responsibilities endemic to the effective and efficient administration of the public's business on the other. Since its inception the character of this Republic has consistently reflected the need for proper balance between rights and responsibilities.[24]

It is difficult to see how maintaining the productivity of the federal bureaucracy requires the sweeping prohibitions on partisan activity embodied in the Hatch Act. If, for instance, political activities during working hours prevented the accomplishment of assigned tasks, then narrow "time, place, and manner" restrictions forbidding such activity could easily be drawn which are no different in intent or effect from similar rules in private industry, or rules prescribing the length of lunch hours or the working day. If, however, the concern were that political activity after working hours would cause an adverse effect during the working day, narrow regulations similar to rules intended to ensure that an employee's proficiency is maintained at a desired level could alleviate that concern. If, finally, the fear were that overt displays of political involvement would create tensions among the employees that would interfere with their work, again, narrowly drawn restraints could prevent such results in much the same way that attempts are made to minimize racial tensions.

Under close examination, therefore, the "efficiency" defense of the Hatch Act falls far short of the persuasiveness required to justify restrictions on First Amendment freedoms. Even if some marginal loss of efficiency were entailed, the general public could not merely for the sake of some undetermined amount of convenience properly deny to federal employees what the public itself retains. If the effectiveness of a governmental program were to be seriously jeopardized because of some degree of political involvement by some of its staff members, then the real question would not be whether the activity should be proscribed, but whether the program itself were at all necessary.

The second value encompassed within the notion of "efficiency" and "professionalism"—that civil servants ought to be divorced from partisan politics without regard to whether any political involvement would adversely affect their work performance—is quite clearly a "good government" argument. That is, the appearance of a pristine and nonpartisan professionalism is at least as important as the actual presence of professionalism. As one representative of a federal union

---

[24] Statement of Dr. Wingfield, p. S 20209. As reprinted, Dr. Wingfield's statement did not include the word "freedom," printed within brackets in the text. His statement would make sense with either "freedom" or a synonym.

opposed to substantial weakening of the Hatch Act testified: "the spectacle of public workers in the Federal departments and agencies up to their eyebrows in partisan political campaigning would tend to increase the criticism and the cynicism which now is so endemic throughout our country."[25] Again, the concern expressed is not the appearance of partiality or coercion, but rather the appearance of politicization standing alone.

Resistance to the appearance of political involvement is an often unarticulated and almost emotional rather than a rational position. It is akin in several respects, although with far less persuasive reason, to the doctrine that judges should be "above politics." Indeed, the argument verges on asserting that it is aesthetically unpleasing to see civil servants involved in partisan campaigns. In a nation even minimally committed to First Amendment values, such a defense of the Hatch Act is patently insufficient. As Mr. Justice Brandeis said, the fear "of serious injury cannot alone justify suppression of free speech and assembly. . . . Those who won our independence were not cowards. They did not fear political change. They did not exalt order at the cost of liberty."[26]

The most severe inadequacy of the "efficiency" rationale is, ironically, that it provides a straw target for opponents of the Hatch Act. The Senate Committee on Post Office and Civil Service recently argued in support of H.R. 8617 that ". . . it does not see the continuance of the merit system in public employment as being dependent upon maintenance of the severe restrictions on employees' first amendment rights that now exist."[27] The committee's argument is convincing, and if "professionalism" and "efficiency" were the most persuasive rationales for the Hatch Act, little reason would exist to preserve that statute.

3. The Coercion of Public Employees

The Sheppard committee's investigations in 1939 revealed several instances of actual or attempted coercion of public employees for political purposes. Certified Works Progress Administration (WPA) employees in Kentucky holding views contrary to those of Senator Alben W. Barkley (Democrat, Kentucky) were discharged after canvassing of such workers by their supervisors.[28] In Tennessee, there

---

[25] Testimony of Dr. Nathan T. Wolkomir in *Hearings on H.R. 3000*, p. 148.

[26] Whitney v. California, 274 U.S. 357, 376-77 (1927) (concurring opinion).

[27] S. Rep. No. 94-512, 94th Congress, 1st session (1974), p. 4.

[28] *Report of the Special Committee*, p. 12.

were substantial efforts to raise campaign funds from federal employees (both from civil service workers and from those on relief), including in some circumstances the use of intimidation and coercion.[29] WPA workers and employees in Pennsylvania were told that there was "no excuse" for not attending a certain political rally in late October 1938.[30] Other WPA workers ("even women on sewing projects" as the Senate committee put it) were ordered to change their voter registration from Republican to Democratic, and several who refused to comply were fired from the WPA.[31] In a Maryland Senate race, an internal revenue collector took a clearly delineated position on behalf of one candidate by reading a prepared statement to his subordinates.[32]

Based on these and other similar findings, supporters of the Hatch Act concluded that federal employees needed protection from coercion and threats of coercion by their supervisors.[33] Opponents of the act argued to the contrary that "it is wrong and un-American for this Congress to legislate to curtail the political right and the political freedom of the WPA employee in my district, who is laboring with a spade for $26 per month."[34] Representative Vito Marcantonio (American Labor Party, N.Y.) warned that the Hatch Act "is a step in seven-league boots toward disenfranchising the unemployed of this country."[35] Hatch Act supporters brushed aside these objections.

---

[29] Ibid., p. 18.

[30] Ibid., p. 24. The Sheppard committee found that the term "no excuse" addressed to WPA workers on relief "is indefensible, and that it is in the nature of an implied threat and a grave interference with the right of relief workers to be free from coercion in the exercise of their political rights." Ibid., p. 25.

[31] Ibid., pp. 25, 27.

[32] Ibid., p. 31.

[33] An enlightening episode during House debate over the Hatch bill corroborates this rationale. Section 6 of the bill (and also of the act) made it unlawful to disclose lists of persons receiving federal aid to political candidates or their associates. Representative Edward Creal (Democrat, Kentucky) proposed to delete the section, stating "I maintain it is a monstrosity to say that we cannot receive such a list, if we want to send our remarks for or against some bill in which they are interested, after having received numerous letters. . . . You cannot in your own county know who is on the WPA or who is on the relief rolls. You may want this information in order to tell them your views on certain legislation in which they are interested." *Congressional Record*, vol. 84 (July 20, 1939), p. 9620. It is, of course, precisely the fact that elected officials or other partisans "told" too much to WPA employees and others that motivated many legislators to support Senator Hatch's bill.

[34] Remarks of Representative Green, *Congressional Record,* vol. 84 (July 20, 1939), p. 9630.

[35] Ibid., p. 9632.

The Supreme Court has consistently relied upon the possibility of employee coercion to uphold the constitutionality of the Hatch Act. Speaking of appellant Poole in the *Mitchell* case, the Court noted that

> if in free time he is engaged in political activity, Congress may have concluded that the activity may promote or retard his advancement or preferment with his superiors. Congress may have thought that government employees are handy elements for leaders in political policy to use in building a political machine. . . . Evidently what Congress feared was the cumulative effect on employee morale of political activity by all employees who could be induced to participate actively.[36]

In *Letter Carriers*, the Court characterized as "the judgment of history" the proposition "that federal service should depend upon meritorious performance rather than political service" and upheld the congressional policy that the bureaucracy ". . . be free from pressure and from express or tacit invitation to vote in a certain way or perform political chores in order to curry favor with their superiors rather than to act out their own beliefs."[37]

The immediate response of many opponents of the Hatch Act—particularly from those union leaders whose power would increase the most if the act's strictures were to be discarded—is that coercion has not been and will not be a problem. Obviously, in their view, the act is neither necessary nor desirable. A second response to the coercion argument is that private employees are just as subject to political pressures as government employees and thus also arguably in need of a Hatch Act to protect them. Mr. Justice Black strongly implied that no such law applicable to private citizens could, in his view, pass constitutional muster.[38] He stressed that if political favoritism rather than merit governed advancement in federal service, that element of bias should be proscribed, just as some state statutes made political coercion of private employees unlawful. In short, in Justice Black's view, federal employees were "second-class citizens" because they were treated differently from workers outside the government.[39]

---

[36] 330 U.S. 75, 101.

[37] 413 U.S. 548, 557, 566.

[38] 330 U.S. 75, 113 (Black, J., dissenting).

[39] The "second-class citizen" argument at times degenerates into simplistic sloganeering, as does so much of the debate over the Hatch Act. During hearings in Cleveland, Ohio, recently, Representative William Clay (Democrat, Missouri)

The notion that coercion is not or would not become a serious problem is one that is quickly disproven, as the WPA experience demonstrates. Moreover, the general counsel of the Civil Service Commission has observed that many federal employees read the Hatch Act very broadly in order to protect themselves from what they perceive to be political pressure. They are able to say "I'm Hatched" even in circumstances to which the act may not apply, and by so doing ward off attempts to have them engage in political activity.[40] While ostensibly disclaiming an intention to intimidate government employees, one official of a union strongly supporting significant modification of the act complained that some "Federal workers really are afraid to get too mixed up in politics, and some Federal employees really hide behind the Hatch Act as a way to get out of participating or voting. . . ."[41] It seems clear that both supporters and opponents of the act fully recognize that it can be and often is used as a shield. We are justifiably concerned when that shield is threatened by random and individualistic threats of coercion; when it is threatened by the organized and comprehensive pressure of public employee unions or supervisory personnel (most likely in an effort to create a political power base), our concern necessarily increases accordingly.

An interesting variation on the argument that coercion will not increase is the contention that there are already so many political activities federal employees may engage in voluntarily (so that, consequently, they are subjected to coercion to engage in precisely those activities), that repeal of the major provisions of the Hatch Act would not alter the existing situation to any considerable degree.[42] This argument, if valid, would properly lead not to the conclusion that the act should be gutted, but that it is underinclusive as written—that not enough activities are prohibited—and that it should be strengthened. Civil servants can currently engage in numerous activities[43] that consistency might indicate should also be prohibited. Mr. Justice Black dismissed such activities as mere "minor exceptions" in *United Public Workers* v. *Mitchell*,[44] and Congress's failure to include them

---

equated the status of federal employees with that of citizens of the Soviet Union, and told one union official opposed to H.R. 3000 that "You are a second-class citizen because of this Hatch Act, whether I convince you of it or not." *Hearings on H.R. 3000*, p. 480.

[40] Statement of Anthony L. Mondello, ibid., p. 33.

[41] Statement of Dennis Garrison, executive vice president of the American Federation of Government Employees, ibid., p. 130.

[42] Ibid., pp. 37–39, 132–33.

[43] See 5 C.F.R., sections 733.111, 733.124.

[44] 330 U.S. 75, 107 n. 4.

within the scope of the Hatch Act may reflect more of a judgment of their political irrelevance than any effort at principled decision making.

The debate has thus isolated a curious paradox: the freer the employees are to engage in voluntary political activity, the greater is the possibility that they will be coerced into involuntary political activity. Hatch Act supporters must thus argue that proscribing certain activities leaves civil servants with more freedom, while its opponents must contend that when those very activities are permitted, civil servants can more easily resist pressure to engage in them.

Supporters of proposals such as H.R. 8617 attempt to avoid this dilemma by arguing that full protection can be afforded to the employees by strengthening the laws against coercion while removing the restraints on truly voluntary partisan involvement.[45] Apart from the fact that such suggestions ignore other arguments in favor of the Hatch Act's broader restraints (see below, Section 4), they provide inadequate protection to the employees. It should be emphasized, moreover, that the employees have a First Amendment right to be free from coercion. It is not merely desirable that they not be coerced; in the governmental context, it is required that they not be coerced.

Restraints on coercion alone force an employee who believes he is being subjected to such coercion to come forward to complain about it, a highly unlikely prospect if that employee is already in fear of his job or his employment future. The only possibly effective method to eliminate coercion is thus to forbid the activity as well as the intimidation. This route (the one followed by the Hatch Act) is strong medicine, to be sure. Nonetheless, there does not appear to be any other equally protective alternative. The Hatch Act as now written is not a perfect solution and Civil Service Commission enforcement may be less than adequate,[46] but it at least provides one more extremely important layer of protection to the employee. The difference between being able to say "I'm Hatched," and "I don't agree with your candidate and I choose not to work for him," is enormously significant, and the degrees of protection involved are far different.

This is not by any means to say that the Hatch Act as written is somehow mandated by the Constitution. It means only that in examining the question of coercion of public employees, it should be borne firmly in mind that there are First Amendment rights on both sides of the issue. There is no a priori reason why one employee's First

---

[45] S. Rep. No. 94-512, p. 5.

[46] Indeed the commission's enforcement activity is now essentially limited only to responding to complaints. *Hearings on H.R. 3000*, pp. 46-47.

Amendment right to engage in partisan activity should be given preference (as repeal of the Hatch Act limitations would do) over his colleague's equally important First Amendment right not to be forced to engage in partisan activity. Of course, there is no a priori reason why the contrary of this proposition is not also valid.

Some would argue, accordingly, that we are left apparently in equipoise, with important First Amendment values on both sides, and with no strong indications of which way to proceed. At this point, opponents of regulation might pose Mr. Justice Black's question— why should public employees be treated differently from private employees? And if they should not be treated differently, does that not provide a strong rationale for not having a Hatch Act?

If the First Amendment is to continue to fulfill its role as a guarantor of government nonintervention in the area of speech and association, the last question should be answered in the negative. In this instance, the Hatch Act does not represent government regulation of citizens so much as it represents government regulating itself. When one federal employee applies political pressure to another, he is in effect applying power vested in his hands by his position in the government. That power comes from the general public, conferred upon the government to perform functions on behalf of the citizens. A federal employee has no more right to use that power for purposes of the political coercion of another employee than an agency of the government has the right to use its power for purposes of political coercion of the general citizenry.

One currently favorable line of defense for congressional supporters of the Hatch Act is that it must be retained to prevent ". . . a power grab by Federal union leaders to place conscientious Federal employees at the mercy and calling of politicians at every level of political activity." [47] To the extent that this statement merely reflects a distaste for powerful labor unions, it is not a constitutionally permissible rationale for regulation. To the extent, however, that it reflects an appreciation of the need that the government not be used as a coercive weapon to induce political involvement, it is completely accurate.

Indeed, the difference between coercion of an employee by a supervisor (the paradigm of 1939) and coercion of an employee by a

---

[47] Minority Views of Representative Edward Derwinski (Republican, Illinois) to H.R. Rep. No. 94-444, 94th Congress, 1st session (1975), reprinted in *Documentary Background to the Federal Employees' Political Activities Act of 1975*, U.S. Senate Committee on Post Office and Civil Service, 94th Congress, 1st session (1975), p. 134.

union—which may include supervisors—(the paradigm of today) is that coercion by a union is far harder to resist. Moreover, it may well be that unions are far more capable of engaging in the systematic solicitation and intimidation of federal employees than a network of supervisors. Public employee unions were not of significant size when the Hatch Act was originally passed, but their advent has, if anything, only made the Hatch Act more important. Union protestations that their presence renders supervisor coercion less likely,[48] however accurate, still provide no answer to the question of what renders union coercion less likely. Those concerned about union political pressure will not find their fears assuaged by the fact that the conventions of three of the most powerful federal employee unions supporting H.R. 3000 were unanimous in their opposition to the Hatch Act as currently written.[49] Nor does the fact that the convention of one union opposed to modification of the Hatch Act was also unanimously for its position [50] do anything to lessen fears of coercion.

The government intervenes to prevent the coercion of federal bureaucrats because not to do so would be in effect to permit the use of federal power to mandate partisan activity. Whatever the permissible grounds of regulation of private employer-employee political relationships, it is clear that some government regulation to protect its own employees from political association enforced against their will is in theory not only consistent with the First Amendment, but virtually required by it.

Theoretical statutes, however, are rarely enacted and the Hatch Act is certainly no constitutional lawyer's Platonic ideal of legislative lawmaking. It is with some uncertainty we can conclude that with respect to preventing the coercion of federal workers, the act as currently written is more desirable than a reform moving in the direction of H.R. 8617. Nevertheless, against a demonstrated historical background of employee coercion, and with the use of public employee unions that represent a potential source of pressure on the individual employee at least as great as that represented by his supervisor, caution in the effective repeal of a statute that has functioned at least adequately is warranted. Such caution is especially justified because the First Amendment rights against coerced political activity of numerous government workers may hang in the balance. The best argument on this question may thus still be that made by Representa-

---

[48] *Hearings on H.R. 3000*, pp. 83–84.

[49] Ibid., pp. 87, 97, 126.

[50] Ibid., p. 140.

tive Robert A. Green (Democrat, Florida) during the 1939 debate: "I am for [the act] because I sincerely believe that it is restoring to millions of WPA workers who have been coerced and abused in recent years their rights as American citizens."[51]

4. "Chilling" the General Public

Conceptually, the political intimidation of the general public is not substantially different from pressure applied to government employees, but the possible adverse consequences are far greater. Moreover, there are additional dangers, according to traditional democratic theory, raised by a politicized bureaucracy that is either overzealous in its loyalties to an administration, or is recalcitrant in carrying out the mandate of elected officials. Thus it is that, as noted previously, the idea of forbidding government workers from engaging in partisan political activity is at bottom a civil libertarian idea—the government is, in effect, restraining itself, and thus in classic First Amendment terms protecting free and voluntary political activity by individuals.

Those who deal with the federal government or those who are significantly affected by it—and in 1976 that surely includes virtually all Americans—must be concerned about the effects of their political opinions and activities when they face federal bureaucrats able to engage in partisan political activity. In constitutional terms, the non-governmental citizen may be "chilled" in his willingness to speak or associate when the consequences of such action may include adverse treatment at the hands of federal officials. Since there "is practically universal agreement that a major purpose of the [First] Amendment was to protect the free discussion of governmental affairs,"[52] it should come as no surprise that restrictions on federal workers' partisan activities are, in their plain effect, restrictions on governmental interference with speech and associational freedoms. As in the case of coercion of government employees, those federal workers who make decisions politically are improperly using power vested in government to serve their own political ends and, most important, doing so at the expense of other citizens. A politically active bureaucracy raises grave dangers that, at least in part, government by the people risks being replaced by government by the government.

There are only a very few indications that Congress in 1939 believed that protection of the individual citizen was a major reason

---

[51] *Congressional Record*, vol. 84 (July 20, 1939), p. 9632.

[52] Mills v. Alabama, 384 U.S. 214, 218 (1966).

for supporting the act.[53] On the contrary, at least some members fully realized the importance of a politically active bureaucracy. Representative Emanuel Celler (Democrat, New York), one of the chief House opponents of Senator Hatch's bill, reminded his colleagues that:

> Fifty Members of the Congress came to the House at the time they were United States attorneys, marshals, or holding a Federal office. They could not have come to the Congress if . . . [the act] were in effect, because they would have been an officeholder, and they could not have taken part in a political campaign.[54]

Representative Elizabeth Holtzman, Representative Celler's successor in the House, has provided the correct rebuttal:

> if there is one lesson we should have learned from Watergate, it is that we must strive to reduce, rather than increase, political influence in the Federal law enforcement and investigative agencies. This bill [H.R. 8617] would, instead, authorize and invite the politicizing of the Justice Department, FBI, U.S. Attorneys' Offices, and Internal Revenue Service, as well as the CIA, National Security Agency and Defense Intelligence Agency.[55]

She posed the hypothetical situations of a U.S. attorney or a district director of Internal Revenue pledged to a particular candidate, and asked how exacting the enforcement of the appropriate statutes against their favored candidate would be.

Equally as deleterious as favoritism to a particular partisan candidate is the possibility for discriminatory enforcement against other candidates or their supporters. Such discrimination could be motivated by distaste for a candidate's philosophy, or from personal, political ambition. Repeal of the Hatch Act's prohibitions against partisan activity would, for instance, allow a United States attorney with political ambitions to enforce the criminal provisions of the Federal Election Campaign Act against an incumbent senator or representative or other potential opponent, and then run for that same office himself as a vindicator of "campaign reform" laws.[56]

---

[53] Colloquy between Representatives Alfred Bulwinkle (Democrat, North Carolina) and James Mott (Republican, Oregon), *Congressional Record*, vol. 84 (July 20, 1939), pp. 9614-15.

[54] Ibid., p. 9597.

[55] *Congressional Record*, vol. 121 (November 18, 1975), p. H 11390.

[56] As passed by the House, H.R. 8617 would amend 5 U.S.C., section 7326 to require federal workers who become candidates to take a ninety-day leave without pay prior to any election in which they are a candidate. The impact of this section

Moreover, fundamental principles of democratic theory are transgressed when the bureaucracy oversteps its limits. Whether it be the use of repression to advance the administration (as in the WPA case, see above Section 3), or the resistance to an administration's policies (as was feared when the post-World War II Labour government assumed power in Great Britain), a politicized civil service would risk violating rules at the core of representative government. Because bureaucrats, particularly higher-level ones, possess established channels of communication to the policy-making organs of the government, they have opportunities to affect decision making to an extent far beyond the ability of the average citizen. If partisan activity were also permitted to them, their influence—as a consequence of the access to federal power provided by their jobs—would be even more disproportionate to that of their fellow citizens.

With partisan activity allowed, government workers would undoubtedly come under more pressure from their partisan colleagues to engage, in effect, in partisan activity on the job, as did WPA officials during the Roosevelt administration. Many in the Nixon administration feared resistance to its initiatives by a hostile bureaucracy. Whether that estimate was correct or not, the partisan proclivities of federal employees would almost certainly be encouraged by permitting them to engage in and be subject to the pressures of partisan activity. Not only would the will of the electorate, as previously expressed, be in danger of transmogrification, but future activity by the electorate would also be interfered with.

Although Representative Holtzman's concern was focused on law-enforcement and intelligence-gathering agencies of the federal government,[57] there is also ample reason to fear the effects politicization would have on citizens who deal with other government bureaus. Other government workers who might have a significant impact on the public include those holding such varied positions as government contracting officer (with the power to grant or deny contracts of

---

is substantially lessened, however, by its provision that such workers may utilize accrued annual leave time to engage in political activity in addition to the ninety-day leave. In any case, the leave provisions do not apply to workers actively engaged in partisan campaigns but who are not themselves candidates.

[57] It was, of course, a law-enforcement officer that caused Mr. Justice (then Judge) Holmes to write that a municipal regulation forbidding members of the police department from soliciting money for political purposes was legitimate and that "the petitioner may have a constitutional right to talk politics, but he has no constitutional right to be a policeman." McCauliffe v. New Bedford, 29 N.E. 517, 517 (Mass. 1892). Hatch Act cases have in fact involved law-enforcement officials; see, for example, Brooks v. Nacrelli, 415 F. 2d 272 (3rd Cir. 1969) (members of a municipal police force alleged to be Republican Party committeemen).

potentially enormous value),[58] official of a federal housing authority,[59] census employee (with access to confidential information),[60] nonpartisan city manager (whose selection of a candidate may determine the availability of federal grants for his city),[61] Federal Trade Commission administrative law judge,[62] and official of the Veterans Administration.[63] The list could go on and on. It was perhaps no accident that the first widely publicized evidence of coercion appeared in the WPA, a welfare agency; with so much of the public dependent on federal subsidies or federal regulation today, the possibilities for coercion are even greater now than at the zenith of the New Deal.

The plain fact is that people do not rigidly compartmentalize their lives; they are, in the main, incapable of being at the same time a neutral government worker by day and a partisan political operative by night. With virtually no limits on federal employees' partisan activity, the deleterious effects of a politicized civil service noted above are almost certain to occur. Although government employees are doubtless not philosophical neuters today, their training and habits discourage the expression of political viewpoints in their work. With the Hatch Act removed, such restraints would be gone. Representative Herbert Harris (Democrat, Virginia) a member of the House Civil Service Committee and a supporter of H.R. 8617, recently stated that:

> I think this person out there who deals in the matters of the Federal Government in his daily life doesn't stop being that type of person when he goes home and his activities in the community are usually very consistent. The notion that this is the type of person who somehow can foreclose himself in the interest of his local government, his community activities, and the State and Federal processes going on around him that influence his life so very intimately I think is a misconception of the type of individual we're dealing with.[64]

That statement can easily be turned around—"the type of individual we're dealing with" does not isolate his daily work from the "processes going on around him" any more than he does the opposite.

---

58 *Hearings on H.R. 3000*, pp. 53–54.

59 Soldevila v. Secretary of Agriculture, 512 F. 2d 427 (1st Cir. 1975).

60 S. Rep. No. 94-444, 94th Congress, 1st session (1975), p. 136 (minority views).

61 Ibid.

62 Remarks of Representative Gilbert Gude (Republican, Maryland) *Congressional Record*, vol. 121 (October 21, 1975), p. H 10130.

63 Ibid.

64 *Hearings on H.R. 3000*, p. 18.

Representative Harris is correct in cautioning us against "misconceptions," but he draws a completely mistaken conclusion from his premise.

Although it appears to be fashionable for some Republicans to oppose measures repealing the Hatch Act's prohibitions on partisan activity by federal workers because of the power of allegedly Democratic-oriented public employee unions, if Congress is to make a legislative judgment purely on the merits of the issue, such partisan attitudes can, of course, play no legitimate part. There is merit, however, in asking whether there is any emphatic direction to the political attitudes that substantial modification of the Hatch Act would release. To the extent that an "un-Hatched" bureaucracy, or a discreet or identifiable segment of it, does have an easily recognizable political or ideological coloration, the "chilling" effect of its partisan activity on the public at large will necessarily be the greater.[65]

As noted previously, when the Hatch Act was passed, large and powerful public employee unions did not exist. Now they do, and the possibilities for concerted action to influence public policy (and therefore the general public) are far greater than they were thirty-five years ago. Just as concern is properly voiced when governmental power is improperly used to coerce federal workers, so too concern is warranted when individuals subject to the government's power are restrained or pressured. The monopoly of legitimate coercive power vested in the government and the access to it by government employees warrant restraints on the government and its workers so that the state's power is not used in unintended ways.

Dissenting in *Broadrick* v. *Oklahoma*, Mr. Justice Douglas applauded a "bureaucracy that is alert, vigilant, and alive" and decried the "suppression of First Amendment rights that creates faceless, nameless bureaucrats who are inert in their localities and submissive to some master's voice."[66] The real concern, however, is "faceless, nameless" citizens "submissive" to the government's voice spoken through its employees. Mr. Justice Douglas was far more accurate in 1947 when he cautioned against "the vast discretionary powers vested in the various agencies, and the impact of their work on

---

[65] The theoretical possibility that the political activity of those with views sympathetic to the bureaucracy will increase in sufficient magnitude to offset the decline in activity of those chilled (so that total political activity will not decline) is insufficient to refute this argument. First Amendment theory is not based on undifferentiated mass activity; it is based on individual right. That some individuals may feel "liberated" by a certain action has never been an adequate justification to repress others.

[66] 413 U.S. 601, 621 (Douglas, J., dissenting).

individual claimants as well as on the general welfare," and warned that "if the incumbents were political adventurers or party workers, partisanship might color or corrupt the processes of administration with which most of the administrative agencies are entrusted."[67] The First Amendment's command that the government not interfere with the people's political debate is thus obeyed when the government restricts itself by precluding partisan political activity by its employees.

Conclusion

Although it has not been frequently made in the past, the best defense of a statute restricting partisan activity by government employees is, in fact, a civil libertarian one. Others that come to mind—such as the prevention of corruption or inefficiency within the civil service— suffer from an insensitivity to the speech and associational rights of those workers who do wish to become involved in political affairs. Without a statute like the Hatch Act, however, the insensitivity to such rights would be borne by the general public and those civil servants who did not wish to engage in partisan politics.

Much of the foregoing may be seen more as a defense of an idealized version of the Hatch Act than of the act itself. Indeed, the act could certainly profit from significant revision. The 1940 amendments added section 15 to the act,[68] defining the phrase "an active part in political management or in political campaigns" to mean those acts the Civil Service Commission had forbidden employees in the competitive civil service to engage in before the 1940 amendments. Although this section survived a constitutional challenge in *Letter Carriers*, Congress could surely do better in defining what exactly it is proscribing.[69] H.R. 8617 is clearly no improvement, because it makes no attempt whatever to define "political activity." In addition, the Civil Service Commission's enforcement authority could be strengthened. Rather than awaiting complaints of coercion, the commission should take preventive steps to avoid having federal workers pressured into involuntary political activity.

Until someone drafts an alternative statute that fully protects both government employees and those who deal with the federal gov-

---

[67] 330 U.S. 75, 121-22 (Douglas, J., dissenting in part).

[68] 5 U.S.C., section 7324(a).

[69] Prior to the interpretation of section 15 in *Letter Carriers*, the problems it caused were discussed perceptively in Henry Rose, "A Critical Look at the Hatch Act," *Harvard Law Review*, vol. 75 (1962), p. 510.

ernment from having their First Amendment rights to express themselves chilled, the Hatch Act, with all its deficiencies, still provides a significant measure of protection. To abandon it completely would risk not only politicizing some elements of the federal bureaucracy, but also chilling the political activities of much of the rest of the nation. A risk so inconsistent with fundamental First Amendment values should not be taken.

Cover and book design: Pat Taylor